Practice Test for the Cognitive Abilities Test (CogAT®*)

Primary Edition (Levels K – 2)

By Mercer Publishing

# Practice Test for the
# Cognitive Abilities Test (CogAT®*)
# Primary Edition (Levels K – 2)

A study aid to help your child get into a gifted program.

Mercer Publishing

* CogAT® is a registered trademark of the Houghton Mifflin Company which was not involved in the production of, and does not endorse, this practice test.

# INTRODUCTION

As a parent and educator, I understand how important it is to ensure your children are given the opportunites they deserve when it comes to their education. One of the greatest opportunities your child will have is entering the gifted program, if they can qualify for the program based on their test scores.

One of the primary tools for measuring a student's ability to enter the gifted program is the Cognative Abilities Test (CogAT®*) published by Riverside Publishing. This test is made up of tests in three areas: Verbal, Quantitative and Nonverbal. Your child's score on this test is likely the sole predictor of their inclusion, or non-inclusion, into the gifted program.

Most resources state that there are really no ways to prepare for this test - that your child should only get a good night's sleep before taking the test. An official practice test with sample questions does exist, but it is only available to licensed test administrators. It is guaranteed that if your child is not familiar with some of the symbols used in the test or if they have never done some of the types of problems before, that they will not do as well as they could on this test – perhaps jepordizing their admission into the gifted program. So what should the average parent do?

If you have purchased this practice test, you have taken the first step. This practice test contains six tests in the three test areas found on the CogAT®* Primary Edition (levels K – 2), which is usually given to students in kindergarten and first grade:

VERBAL

| | |
|---|---|
| Oral Vocabulary | 20 questions |
| Verbal Reasoning | 20 questions |

QUANTITATIVE

| | |
|---|---|
| Relational Concepts | 20 questions |
| Quantitative Concepts | 20 questions |

NONVERBAL

| | |
|---|---|
| Figure Classification | 20 questions |
| Matrices | 20 questions |

The object of this practice test is to familiarize your child with the types of questions they will face on test day, how the tests are formatted, the symbols used and the number of questions in each test area. However, since this practice test has not been standardized with Riverside Publishing and the actual CogAT®* test, a valid CogAT®* test score cannot be concluded from their results on this practice test.

Good luck on this practice test and your upcoming CogAT®* test.

Mercer Publishing

# TABLE OF CONTENTS

# TEST TAKING INFORMATION

The Cognitive Abilities Test (CogAT®*) Primary Edition, which is usually given to students in kindergarten and first grade, is an untimed, multiple choice test. Questions are read to the students by a test administrator and the students make their answer selections in the test booklet. The questions are read only once.

The official guideline from the publisher is that students should not guess if they do not know the answer – that random guessing compromises the validity of the scores. However, the CogAT®* score is calculated based on the number of right answers and the student is not penalized for incorrect answers. As a parent looking for a high score, it is better for your child to answer all questions than leave an answer blank.

There are some approaches to standardized testing that have been proven to increase test scores. Review the following strategies with your child and have them practice these as they go through the practice test.

**Listen Carefully.** Instructions will be given to your child during the exam, including directions for each section and how to fill out the test forms. Many errors are made because children do not listen to the instructions as carefully as they should. If your child fills in the answers incorrectly or marks in the wrong section, your child's score will be lowered significantly.

**Listen to the Entire Question.** Some children begin filling in answers before they finish hearing the entire question. It could be that the last part of the question has the information needed to answer the question correctly.

**Look at all the Available Answers.** In their desire to finish quickly or first, many children select the first answer that seems right to them without reading all of the answers and choosing the one that best answers the question. No additional points are given for finishing the test early. Make sure your child understands the importance of evaluating all the answers before choosing one.

**Eliminate Answer Choices.** If your child can eliminate one or more of the answer choices as definitely wrong, their chances of guessing correctly among the remaining choices improve their odds of getting the answer right.

Now, on to the practice test.

# ORAL VOCABULARY

Each question in this section is read to the student taking the test by a test administrator. The question will ask the student to select the picture best represented by the vocabulary word. The student fills in the circle under the picture they have selected as their answer.

20 questions
Approximate time to complete: 22 minutes

1. Select the picture below that shows the owl.

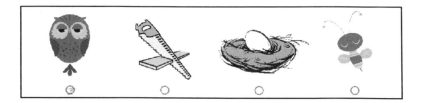

2. Select the picture below that shows the nurse.

3. Select the picture below that shows the camel.

4. Select the picture below that shows the tractor.

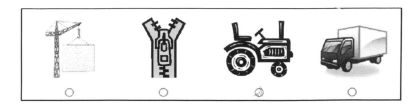

5. Select the picture below that shows the goose.

6. Select the picture below that shows the foot.

7. Select the picture below that shows the orange.

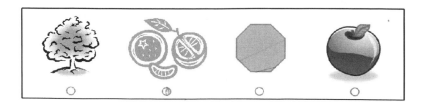

8. Select the picture below that shows the pot.

9. Select the picture below that shows the lock.

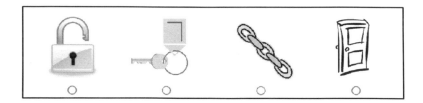

10. Select the picture below that shows the letter.

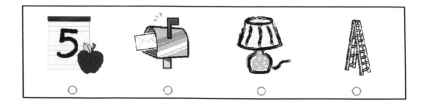

11. Select the picture below that shows the deck.

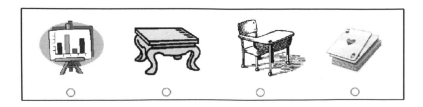

12. Select the picture below that shows the bowl.

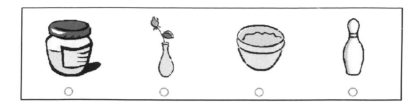

13. Select the picture below that shows the mitten.

14. Select the picture below that shows the dart.

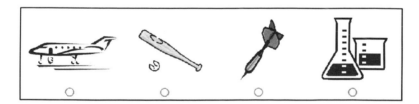

15. Select the picture below that shows the cone.

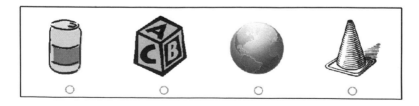

16. Select the picture below that shows the berry.

17. Select the picture below that shows the aquarium.

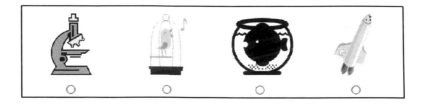

18. Select the picture below that shows the brook.

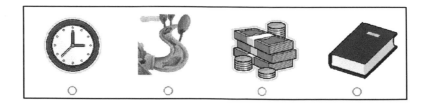

19. Select the picture below that shows the fireworks.

20.  Select the picture below that shows the yarn.

# VERBAL REASONING

In each of the questions in this section, a test administrator reads some information and asks the student a question. The student will need to think about the information that is provided and select the picture that best answers the question. The student fills in the circle under the picture they have selected as their answer.

20 questions
Approximate time to complete: 24 minutes

1. Billy sat down to have lunch. He is having soup today. What should he use to eat it?

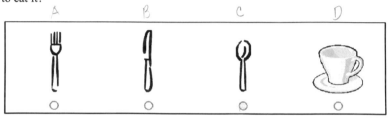

2. John is going to make a birdhouse. He has the wood and the nails, but he still needs something else. What is it?

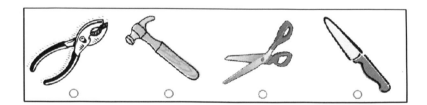

3. Mrs. Frank will make a salad for dinner. When she goes to the store, what will she need to buy?

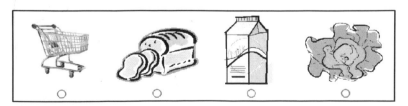

4. Holly sat down to write a story. What will she need?

5. Matthew's bike has a flat tire. When his father went to the garage to fix it, what did he use?

6. Fred was going to his uncle's farm. While he was there, what might he be able to ride?

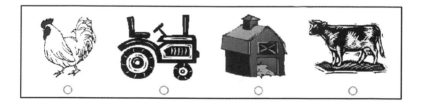

7. Mary's grandmother was teaching her to knit a sweater. What did Mary need?

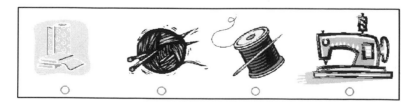

8. Kevin was at the store and wanted a piece of candy. His mother said he could get it and gave him something to pay for it. What was it?

      O         O         O         O

9. The sign was so far away that Mr. Peterson could not read the letters. What could he use to see it?

      O         O         O         O

10. At the orchard, Suzie got to pick the fruit right off the tree. What did she pick?

      O         O         O         O

11. It is getting dark and an eagle is heading home to go to sleep. Where would the eagle go?

      O         O         O         O

12. Michael and Jeffrey are preparing to go on a hike. They get water, a map and sunscreen. What will they use to carry their things on the hike?

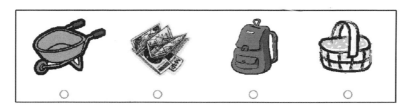

13. The kindergarten class is going on a fieldtrip to the zoo. What animal is Carson looking forward to seeing on the fieldtrip?

14. Mr. Johnson is a famous musician. He often performs on stage in front of a large audience. What is his instrument?

15. It is raining outside so I should remember to take something so I don't get wet. What is it?

16. Mr. Beasley is an engineer. What does he drive at work?

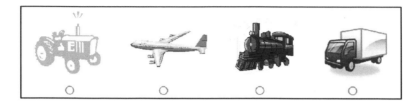

17. It was Brian's birthday. His mom brought in his present. It was in a basket under a small blanket. The blanket began to move and Brian heard a little bark. What was his present?

18. It is cold outside. Karen should dress warmly. First, she puts on her coat. What else should she put on?

19. George came home from school and wanted a snack. His mother said he could have a snack as long as it was not something sweet. George had an idea for something his mother would allow. What was it?

20.  It was getting late and it was almost dark.  They had a long way to walk before they got home.  What should they use to help them see?

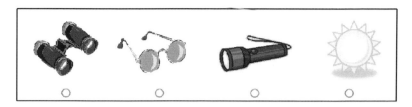

# RELATIONAL CONCEPTS

Each question in this section is read to the student taking the test by a test administrator. The question will ask the student to select the picture best represented by the relational concept. The student fills in the circle under the picture they have selected as their answer.

20 questions
Approximate time to complete: 21 minutes

1. Select the picture below that shows something full.

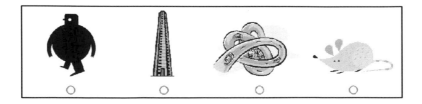

2. Select the picture that shows something slow.

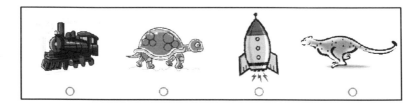

3. Select the picture below that shows something tall.

4. Select the picture below that shows something upside down.

5. Select the picture below that shows something quiet.

6. Select the picture below that shows many.

7. Select the picture below that shows something up.

8. Select the picture below that shows something inside.

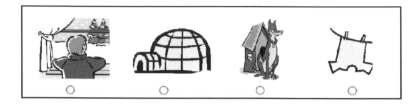

9. Select the picture below that shows something that is not cold.

10. Select the picture below that shows something that is not black and white.

11. Select the picture below that shows something opposite.

12. Select the picture below that shows the kitten on something.

13. Select the picture below that shows the girl in front of something.

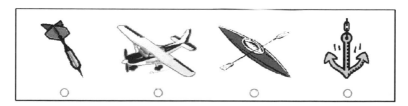

14. Select the picture below of the object that floats.

15. Select the picture below of the heaviest item.

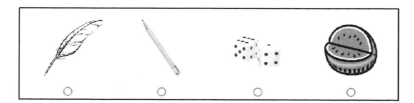

16. Select the picture below of the thing that is farthest away.

17. Select the picture below of the one not on the bicycle.

18. Select the picture below of the one who would have the most candles on their birthday cake.

19. Select the picture below that has the same number of both objects.

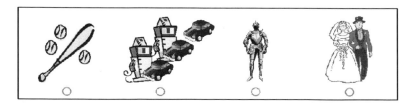

20. Select the picture below that is least like a ball.

# QUANTITATIVE CONCEPTS

Each question in this section has a picture and a set of available answers. The test administrator will read the question to the student, asking them to identify a specific quantity of items in relation to the first picture. The quantity may be more, less or the same as the first picture. The student will count the number of items in the first picture and determine the best available answer. The student fills in the circle under the picture they have selected as their answer.

20 questions
Approximate time to complete: 21 minutes

1.  Count how many triangles are in the first picture. Which one of the other pictures shows 1 more triangle than the first picture?

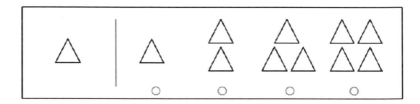

2.  Count how many hearts are in the first picture. Which one of the other pictures shows the same number of hearts as the first picture.

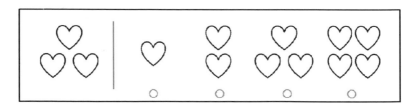

3. Count how many squares are in the first picture. Which one of the other pictures shows 2 more squares than the first picture.

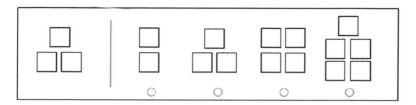

4. Count how many stars are in the first picture. Which one of the other pictures shows 3 more stars than the first picture.

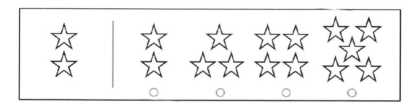

5. Count how many circles are in the first picture. Which one of the other pictures shows 1 more circle than the first picture.

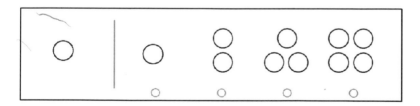

6. Count how many squares are in the first picture. Which one of the other pictures shows 2 less squares than the first picture.

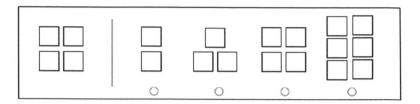

7. Count how many arrows are in the first picture. Which one of the other pictures shows the same number of arrows as the first picture.

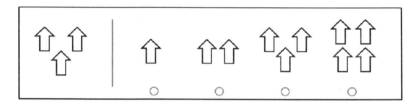

8. Count how many triangles are in the first picture. Which one of the other pictures shows 1 less triangle than the first picture.

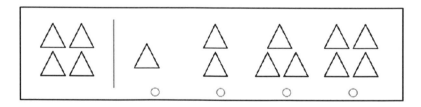

9. Count how many circles are in the first picture. Which one of the other pictures shows 3 less circles than the first picture.

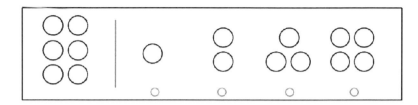

10. Count how many stars are in the first picture. Which one of the other pictures shows 2 less stars than the first picture?

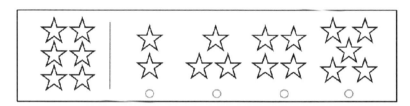

11. Count how many hearts are in the first picture. Which one of the other pictures shows the same number of hearts as the first picture?

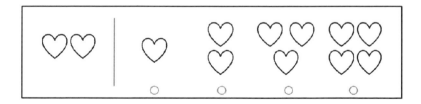

12. Count how many arrows are in the first picture. Which one of the other pictures shows 1 less arrow than the first picture?

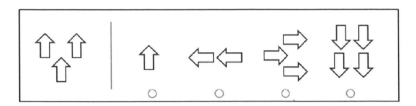

13. Count how many triangles are in the first picture. Which one of the other pictures shows 2 more triangles than the first picture?

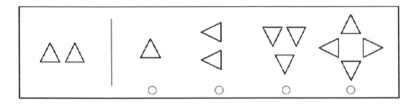

14. Count how many circles are in the first picture. Which one of the other pictures shows 3 less circles than the first picture?

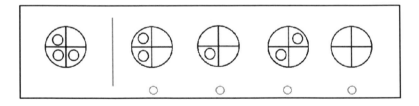

15. Count how many squares are in the first picture. Which one of the other pictures shows 2 less squares than the first picture?

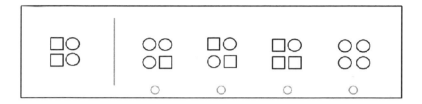

16. Count how many circles are in the first picture. Which one of the other pictures shows 1 more circle than the first picture?

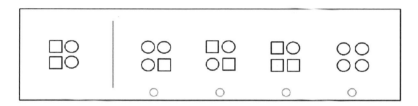

17. Count how many circles are in the first picture. Which one of the other pictures shows 1 more circle than the first picture?

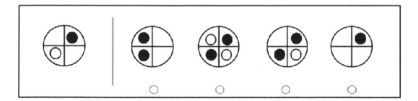

18. Count how many sides are in the first shape. Which one of the other pictures shows a shape with 1 less side than the first picture?

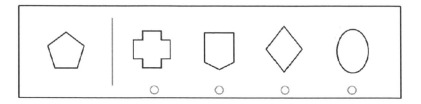

19. Count all the shapes are in the first picture. Which one of the other pictures shows 2 more shapes than the first picture?

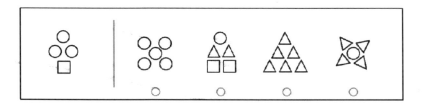

20. Count all the shapes in the first picture. Which one of the other pictures shows the same number of shapes as the first picture?

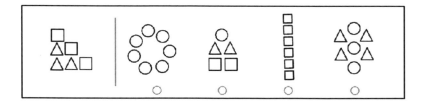

# FIGURE CLASSIFICATION

In this test section, the student will review the first three pictures in each question and determine why they are similar. They will select the picture from the available answers that is most similar to the first three pictures and fill in the circle below their answer.

20 questions
Approximate time to complete: 22 minutes

1. Look at the first three pictures. How are they alike? Look at the answer choices and choose the picture that is most similar to the first three pictures.

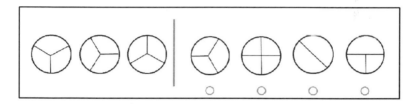

2. Look at the first three pictures. How are they alike? Look at the answer choices and choose the picture that is most similar to the first three pictures.

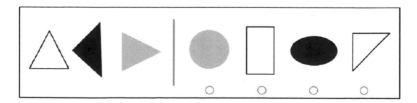

3. Look at the first three pictures. How are they alike? Look at the answer choices and choose the picture that is most similar to the first three pictures.

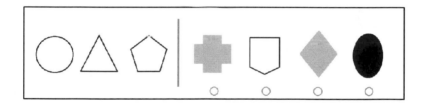

4. Look at the first three pictures. How are they alike? Look at the answer choices and choose the picture that is most similar to the first three pictures.

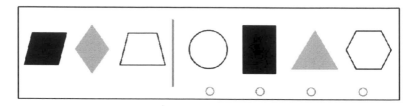

○      ○      ○      ○

5. Look at the first three pictures. How are they alike? Look at the answer choices and choose the picture that is most similar to the first three pictures.

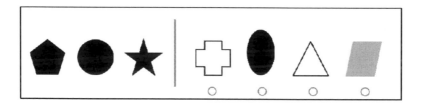

○      ○      ○      ○

6. Look at the first three pictures. How are they alike? Look at the answer choices and choose the picture that is most similar to the first three pictures.

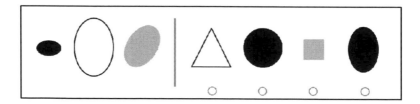

○      ○      ○      ○

7. Look at the first three pictures. How are they alike? Look at the answer choices and choose the picture that is most similar to the first three pictures.

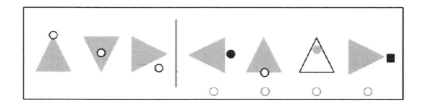

8. Look at the first three pictures. How are they alike? Look at the answer choices and choose the picture that is most similar to the first three pictures.

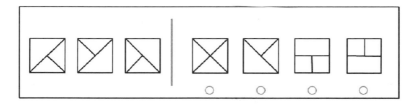

9. Look at the first three pictures. How are they alike? Look at the answer choices and choose the picture that is most similar to the first three pictures.

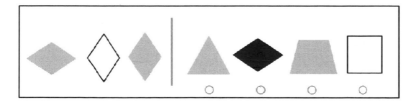

10. Look at the first three pictures. How are they alike? Look at the answer choices and choose the picture that is most similar to the first three pictures.

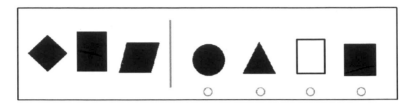

11. Look at the first three pictures. How are they alike? Look at the answer choices and choose the picture that is most similar to the first three pictures.

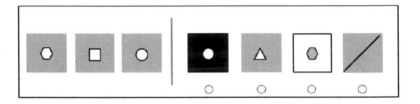

12. Look at the first three pictures. How are they alike? Look at the answer choices and choose the picture that is most similar to the first three pictures.

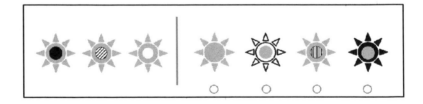

13. Look at the first three pictures. How are they alike? Look at the answer choices and choose the picture that is most similar to the first three pictures.

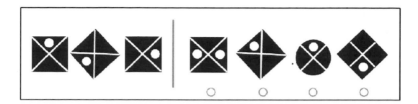

14. Look at the first three pictures. How are they alike? Look at the answer choices and choose the picture that is most similar to the first three pictures.

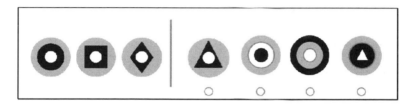

15. Look at the first three pictures. How are they alike? Look at the answer choices and choose the picture that is most similar to the first three pictures.

16. Look at the first three pictures. How are they alike? Look at the answer choices and choose the picture that is most similar to the first three pictures.

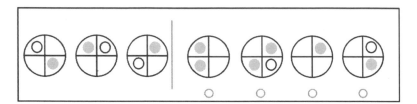

17. Look at the first three pictures. How are they alike? Look at the answer choices and choose the picture that is most similar to the first three pictures.

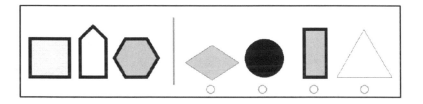

18. Look at the first three pictures. How are they alike? Look at the answer choices and choose the picture that is most similar to the first three pictures.

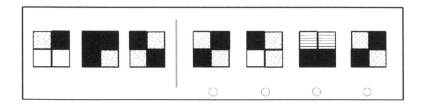

19. Look at the first three pictures. How are they alike? Look at the answer choices and choose the picture that is most similar to the first three pictures.

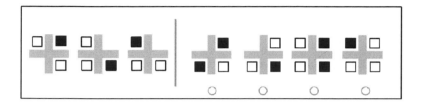

20. Look at the first three pictures. How are they alike? Look at the answer choices and choose the picture that is most similar to the first three pictures.

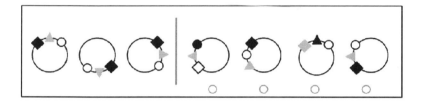

# MATRICES

Each question in this test area has a square that is divided into four sections. The student will review the pictures in the top two sections and determine if they are alike or different. If they are different, they should determine how or why they are different - in some questions they will be moved or modified in some way – or how they go together.

The bottom two sections contain a picture and a blank. Using the same relationship as the top two pictures, the student will select the picture from the available answers that would best complete the matrix. The student fills in the circle under the picture they have selected as their answer.

20 questions
Approximate time to complete: 22 minutes

1. Look at the top two pictures. The first picture is a circle and the second picture is a circle. Are they alike or different? How are they different? Now look at the picture in the bottom row. It is a triangle. To complete the matrix, look at the answer choices and choose the picture that goes with the triangle the same way the first two pictures go together.

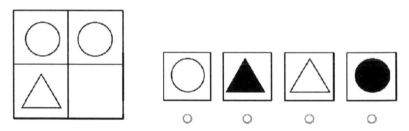

2. Look at the top two pictures.  The first picture is a cross and the second picture is a cross.  Are they alike or different?  How are they different?  Now look at the picture in the bottom row.  It is a diamond.  To complete the matrix, look at the answer choices and choose the picture that goes with the diamond the same way the first two pictures go together.

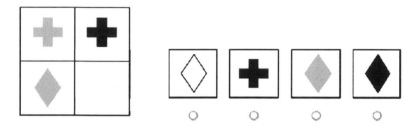

3. Look at the top two pictures.  The first picture is two circles and the second picture is two circles.  Are they alike or different?  How are they different?  Now look at the picture in the bottom row.  It is a star.  To complete the matrix, look at the answer choices and choose the picture that goes with the star the same way the first two pictures go together.

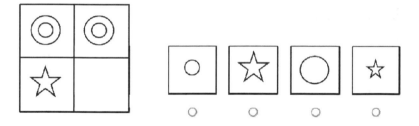

4. Look at the top two pictures. The first picture is a square and the second picture is a square with a circle inside. Are they alike or different? How are they different? Now look at the picture in the bottom row. It is a triangle. To complete the matrix, look at the answer choices and choose the picture that goes with the triangle the same way the first two pictures go together.

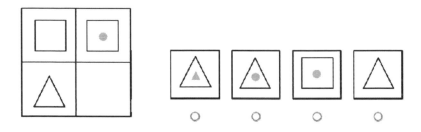

5. Look at the top two pictures. The first picture is a circle with an X and two circles in the middle and the second picture is a circle with an X and one circle in the middle. Are they alike or different? How are they different? Now look at the picture in the bottom row. It is a square with a line and two circles. To complete the matrix, look at the answer choices and choose the picture that goes with the triangle the same way the first two pictures go together.

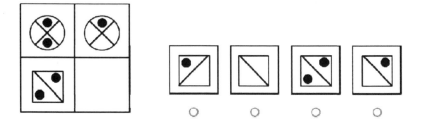

6. Look at the top two pictures. The first picture is a circle with an X and the second picture is two circles with an X. Are they alike or different? How are they different? Now look at the picture in the bottom row. It is a triangle. To complete the matrix, look at the answer choices and choose the picture that goes with the triangle the same way the first two pictures go together.

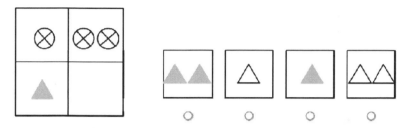

7. Look at the top two pictures. The first picture is a circle and the second picture is a circle with an X. Are they alike or different? How are they different? Now look at the picture in the bottom row. It is a square. To complete the matrix, look at the answer choices and choose the picture that goes with the square the same way the first two pictures go together.

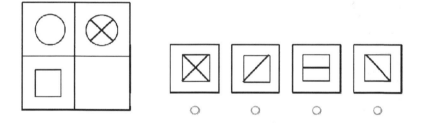

8. Look at the top two pictures. The first picture is a flower and the second picture is a flower. Are they alike or different? How are they different? Now look at the picture in the bottom row. It is a flower. To complete the matrix, look at the answer choices and choose the picture that goes with the flower on the bottom the same way the first two pictures go together.

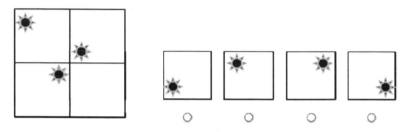

9. Look at the top two pictures. The first picture is a circle and the second picture is a circle. Are they alike or different? How are they different? Now look at the picture in the bottom row. It is a moon. To complete the matrix, look at the answer choices and choose the picture that goes with the moon the same way the first two pictures go together.

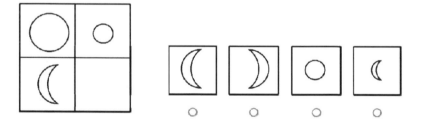

10. Look at the top two pictures. The first picture is a heart and the second picture is a heart. Are they alike or different? How are they different? Now look at the picture in the bottom row. It is a square. To complete the matrix, look at the answer choices and choose the picture that goes with the square the same way the first two pictures go together.

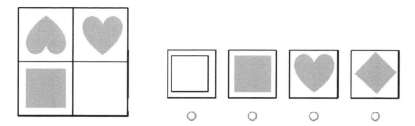

11. Look at the top two pictures. The first picture is two X and the second picture is one X. Are they alike or different? How are they different? Now look at the picture in the bottom row. It is three triangles. To complete the matrix, look at the answer choices and choose the picture that goes with the three triangles the same way the first two pictures go together.

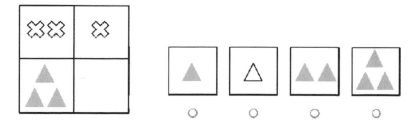

12.  Look at the top two pictures.  The first picture is a circle and the second picture is an oval.  Are they alike or different?  How are they different?  Now look at the picture in the bottom row.  It is a square.  To complete the matrix, look at the answer choices and choose the picture that goes with the square the same way the first two pictures go together.

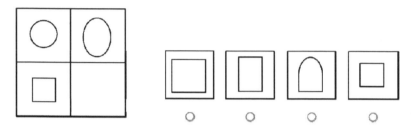

13. Look at the top two pictures.  The first picture is a triangle and the second picture is a triangle.  Are they alike or different?  How are they different?  Now look at the picture in the bottom row.  It is a rectangle.  To complete the matrix, look at the answer choices and choose the picture that goes with the rectangle the same way the first two pictures go together.

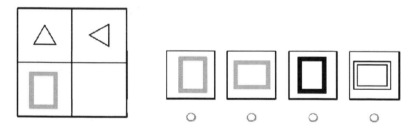

14. Look at the top two pictures. The first picture is a square with two circles and the second picture is a square with two circles. Are they alike or different? How are they different? Now look at the picture in the bottom row. It is a triangle with a small triangle in it. To complete the matrix, look at the answer choices and choose the picture that goes with the triangle the same way the first two pictures go together.

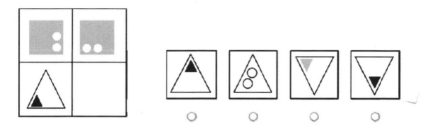

15. Look at the top two pictures. The first picture is a circle with a rectangle and the second picture is a circle with a rectangle. Are they alike or different? How are they different? Now look at the picture in the bottom row. It is two triangles. To complete the matrix, look at the answer choices and choose the picture that goes with the two triangles the same way the first two pictures go together.

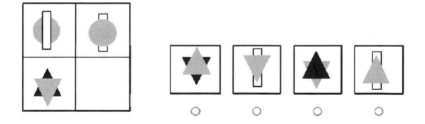

16. Look at the top two pictures. The first picture is two squares and two circles and the second picture is two squares and two circles. Are they alike or different? How are they different? Now look at the picture in the bottom row. It is a half circle. To complete the matrix, look at the answer choices and choose the picture that goes with the half circle the same way the first two pictures go together.

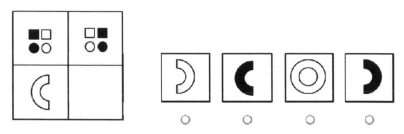

17. Look at the top two pictures. The first picture is a triangle and the second picture is a square. Are they alike or different? How are they different? Now look at the picture in the bottom row. It is a square. To complete the matrix, look at the answer choices and choose the picture that goes with the square the same way the first two pictures go together.

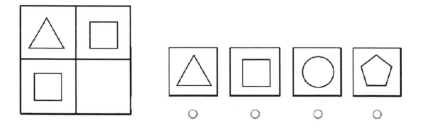

18. Look at the top two pictures. The first picture is a hat and the second picture is a head. These pictures go together in some way. How do they go together? Now look at the picture in the bottom row. It is cherries. To complete the matrix, look at the answer choices and choose the picture that goes with the cherries the same way the first two pictures go together.

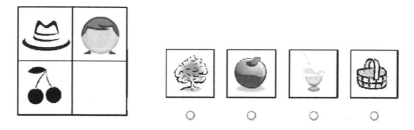

19. Look at the top two pictures. The first picture is snow and the second picture is a snowman. These pictures go together in some way. How do they go together? Now look at the picture in the bottom row. It is flour. To complete the matrix, look at the answer choices and choose the picture that goes with the flour the same way the first two pictures go together.

20. Look at the top two pictures. The first picture is a basketball and the second picture is skis. These pictures go together in some way. How do they go together? Now look at the picture in the bottom row. It is a banana. To complete the matrix, look at the answer choices and choose the picture that goes with the banana the same way the first two pictures go together.

○          ○          ○          ○

# ANSWERS

ORAL VOCABULARY

1. Owl
2. Nurse
3. Camel
4. Tractor
5. Goose
6. Foot
7. Orange (the second answer)
8. Flower Pot
9. Padlock
10. Mailbox
11. Deck of Cards
12. Bowl (the third answer)
13. Mittens
14. Dart
15. Construction Cone
16. Strawberry
17. Fishbowl
18. Brook/Stream
19. Fireworks
20. Yarn and Knitting Needles

## VERBAL REASONING

1. Spoon
2. Hammer
3. Lettuce
4. Pencil
5. Air Pump
6. Tractor
7. Yarn and Knitting Needles
8. Coins
9. Binoculars
10. Apple
11. Nest
12. Backpack
13. Lion
14. Piano
15. Umbrella
16. Train
17. Puppy
18. Scarf
19. Popcorn
20. Flashlight

# RELATIONAL CONCEPTS

1. Full Box (the fourth answer)
2. Turtle
3. Building
4. Acrobat (the third answer)
5. Rabbit
6. Marbles
7. Girl with Hand Raised
8. Child Looking Out Window
9. Sled
10. Cat
11. Chef Looking in Mirror
12. Kitten on the Table
13. Girl with Her Parents
14. Boat/Kayak
15. Watermelon
16. Moon
17. Girl on the Tricycle (the first answer)
18. Oldest Lady (the third answer)
19. Bride and Groom
20. Coins

## QUANTITATIVE CONCEPTS

1. Two Triangles
2. Three Hearts
3. Five Squares
4. Five Stars
5. Two Circles
6. Two Squares
7. Three Arrows
8. Three Triangles
9. Three Circles
10. Four Stars
11. Two Hearts
12. Two Arrows
13. Four Triangles
14. Circle with One Inside Circle (The Second Answer)
15. Four Circles (The Fourth Answer)
16. Three Circles and One Square (The First Answer)
17. Circle with Three Inside Circles (The Third Answer)
18. Diamond
19. Six Triangles
20. Six Squares

FIGURE CLASSIFICATION

1. The first answer. The first three pictures are all rotations of the same object.
2. The second answer. The first three pictures are white.
3. The fourth answer. The first three pictures are all triangles.
4. The second answer. The first three pictures are all four sided shapes.
5. The second answer. The first three pictures are all black shapes.
6. The fourth answer. The first three pictures are all ovals. The size, rotation and color are not factors.
7. The second answer. The first three pictures are a large triangle and a small circle. The rotation and position are not factors.
8. The second answer. The first three pictures are the same shape rotated.
9. The second answer. The first three pictures are diamonds – the color and rotation are not factors.
10. The fourth answer. The first three pictures are black four-sided objects.
11. The second answer. The three pictures show a square with a white shape on the inside.
12. The third answer. The first three pictures show a sun with a colored circle in the center.
13. The second answer. The first three pictures show the same figure rotated.
14. The first answer. The first three pictures each have an outer circle and a white inner circle with different black shapes between them.
15. The fourth answer. The first three pictures have two shapes that are mirror images of each other.
16. The fourth answer. The first three pictures have one small white circle and one small shaded circle, although in any order.
17. The third answer. The first three pictures have thick borders.
18. The second answer. The first three pictures have different numbers of shaded and lined squares, but all of the lined squares are lined in the same direction (from the top left to the bottom right).
19. The second answer. The first three pictures have a cross with two small white squares and one black square in any order.
20. The fourth answer. The first three pictures have a circle with three small figures – a black square, shaded triangle and white circle, from left to right.

MATRICES

1. The third answer. The first two pictures are the same. The white triangle is the same as the bottom picture.
2. The fourth answer. The second picture on top is the first picture colored black. The black diamond is the picture on the bottom colored black.
3. The second answer. The first two pictures are the same. The large white star is the same as the bottom picture.
4. The second answer. The second picture on top is the first picture with a circle in the middle. The triangle with a circle in the middle shows the same relationship.
5. The fourth answer. One of the black circles is removed in the second picture on top. When one black circle is removed from the picture on the bottom, you get the fourth answer. The first answer is not correct because the figure has the removal of the circle but is also rotated, which is not the same relationship as the top pictures.
6. The first answer. The second picture on top shows one more circle with an X. The two triangle answer shows one more triangle than the bottom picture.
7. The first answer. The second picture on the top shows the first picture with an X in it. When an X is added to the square, you get the first answer.
8. The fourth answer. The second picture on the top shows the flower moved directly down in relation to the first picture. When the flower in the bottom picture is moved directly down, it is moved to the bottom right corner.
9. The fourth answer. The second picture on top is a smaller version of the first picture. The small moon is a smaller version of the large moon on the bottom.
10. The second answer. The top two pictures show the heart flipped over. The shaded square, although not different from the picture on the bottom, shows the same relationship.
11. The third answer. The second picture on top shows one less X. The two triangle answer shows one less triangle than the bottom picture.
12. The second answer. The oval is an elongated circle. The rectangle is an elongated square.
13. The second answer. The second picture on top shows the first triangle rotated 90 degrees counterclockwise. The shaded rectangle on its side shows a 90 degree counterclockwise rotation of the bottom picture.
14. The first answer. The second picture on top is the first picture rotated clockwise one side. The first answer shows the triangle on the bottom rotated clockwise one side.

15. The third answer. The order of the circle and the rectangle are reversed in the top two pictures. The third answer shows the two triangles in reverse order.

16. The first answer. The top two pictures are mirror images of each other. The white half circle is a mirror image of the bottom picture.

17. The fourth answer. The square has one more side than the triangle. The pentagon has one more side than the square.

18. The third answer. A hat is put on top of a head. Cherries are put on top of a sundae.

19. The first answer. The snowman is made from snow. Bread is made from flour.

20. The fourth answer. The basketball and skis are both sports equipment – the same category. The banana is a fruit as are the grapes. The bunch of bananas is not correct because the bunch is more than one of the first picture, which is not the same relationship as the top pictures.

NOTES

# MERCER PUBLISHING

Mercer Publishing understands how important it is to ensure your children are given the opportunities they deserve when it comes to their education. One of the greatest opportunities your child will have is entering the gifted program, if they can qualify for the program based on their test scores.

We provide practice test books for gifted program entry exams that offer:

- Similar questions and test formats to the actual tests
- Full length practice tests
- Answer keys

These books are invaluable tools for your child to score their best - and get into the gifted program!

Please visit our website to find out the current gifted program exams that are available.

WWW.MERCERPUBLISHING.COM